4.48 Psychosis

Sarah Kane

'Kane's dense allegorical language moves effortlessly around the corridors of institutionalised insanity and the journey is deft, brilliant and unnerving in the extreme.' *Time Out*

'A masterpiece of mental and emotional extremity . . . an act of artistic heroism.' *Daily Telegraph*

'A remarkably lucid, gallows-grim record of inner hell and disintegration' *Herald*

Sarah Kane was born in 1971. Her first play *Blasted* was produced at the Royal Court Theatre Upstairs in 1995. Her second play, *Phaedra's Love*, was produced at the Gate Theatre in 1996. In April 1998, *Cleansed* was produced at the Royal Court Theatre Downstairs and in September 1998, *Crave* was produced by Paines Plough and Bright Ltd at the Traverse Theatre, Edinburgh. Her last play, *4.48 Psychosis*, premiered at the Royal Court Jerwood Theatre Upstairs in June 2000. Her short film *Skin*, produced by British Screen/Channel Four, premiered in June 1997. Sarah Kane died in 1999.

T0262517

Methuen Drama

Published by Methuen Drama

7 9 10 8 6

This edition first published in Great Britain in 2002 by
Methuen Publishing Ltd

Reprinted in 2006 by Methuen Drama

Methuen Drama
A & C Black Publishers Limited
38 Soho Square
London W1D 3HB

4.48 Psychosis first published in 2000 by Methuen,
copyright © 2000 Sarah Kane

Sarah Kane has asserted her rights under the Copyright, Designs and Patents
Act, 1988, to be identified as the author of this work.

A CIP catalogue record for this book
is available from the British Library

ISBN: 978-0-413-74830-0

Typeset by Deltatype Ltd, Birkenhead
Printed and bound in Great Britain by
Cox & Wyman Ltd, Reading, Berkshire

Caution

4.48 Psychosis

4.48 Psychosis was first performed at the Royal Court Jerwood Theatre Upstairs, London, on 23 June 2000. The cast was as follows:

Daniel Evans
Jo McInnes
Madeleine Potter

Directed by James Macdonald
Designed by Jeremy Herbert
Lighting by Nigel J Edwards
Sound by Paul Arditti

(*A very long silence.*)

—　But you have friends.

(*A long silence.*)

You have a lot of friends.
What do you offer your friends to make them so
supportive?

(*A long silence.*)

What do you offer your friends to make them so
supportive?

(*A long silence.*)

What do you offer?

(*Silence.*)

— — — — —

a consolidated consciousness resides in a darkened banqueting
hall near the ceiling of a mind whose floor shifts as ten
thousand cockroaches when a shaft of light enters as all
thoughts unite in an instant of accord body no longer expellent
as the cockroaches comprise a truth which no one ever utters

　　I had a night in which everything was revealed to me.
　　How can I speak again?

the broken hermaphrodite who trusted hermself alone finds the
room in reality teeming and begs never to wake from the
nightmare

and they were all there
every last one of them
and they knew my name
as I scuttled like a beetle along the backs of their chairs

Remember the light and believe the light

An instant of clarity before eternal night

don't let me forget

– – – –

I am sad

I feel that the future is hopeless and that things cannot improve

I am bored and dissatisfied with everything

I am a complete failure as a person

I am guilty, I am being punished

I would like to kill myself

I used to be able to cry but now I am beyond tears

I have lost interest in other people

I can't make decisions

I can't eat

I can't sleep

I can't think

I cannot overcome my loneliness, my fear, my disgust

I am fat

I cannot write

I cannot love

My brother is dying, my lover is dying, I am killing them both

I am charging towards my death

I am terrified of medication

I cannot make love

I cannot fuck

I cannot be alone

I cannot be with others

My hips are too big

I dislike my genitals

At 4.48
when desperation visits
I shall hang myself
to the sound of my lover's breathing

I do not want to die

I have become so depressed by the fact of my mortality that I
have decided to commit suicide

I do not want to live

I am jealous of my sleeping lover and covet his induced unconsciousness

When he wakes he will envy my sleepless night of thought and speech unslurred by medication

I have resigned myself to death this year

Some will call this self-indulgence
(they are lucky not to know its truth)
Some will know the simple fact of pain

This is becoming my normality

– – – – –

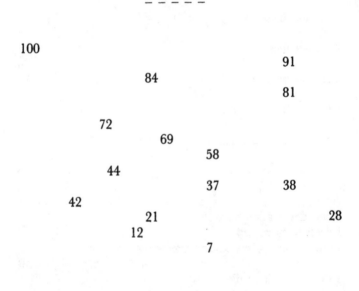

– – – – –

It wasn't for long, I wasn't there long. But drinking bitter black coffee I catch that medicinal smell in a cloud of ancient tobacco and something touches me in that still sobbing place and a wound from two years ago opens like a cadaver and a long buried shame roars its foul decaying grief.

A room of expressionless faces staring blankly at my pain, so devoid of meaning there must be evil intent.

Dr This and Dr That and Dr Whatsit who's just passing and thought he'd pop in to take the piss as well. Burning in a hot tunnel of dismay, my humiliation complete as I shake without reason and stumble over words and have nothing to say about my 'illness' which anyway amounts only to knowing that there's no point in anything because I'm going to die. And I am deadlocked by that smooth psychiatric voice of reason which tells me there is an objective reality in which my body and mind are one. But I am not here and never have been. Dr This writes it down and Dr That attempts a sympathetic murmur. Watching me, judging me, smelling the crippling failure oozing from my skin, my desperation clawing and all-consuming panic drenching me as I gape in horror at the world and wonder why everyone is smiling and looking at me with secret knowledge of my aching shame.

Shame shame shame.
Drown in your fucking shame.

Inscrutable doctors, sensible doctors, way-out doctors, doctors you'd think were fucking patients if you weren't shown proof otherwise, ask the same questions, put words in my mouth, offer chemical cures for congenital anguish and cover each other's arses until I want to scream for you, the only doctor who ever touched me voluntarily, who looked me in the eye, who laughed at my gallows humour spoken in the voice from the newly-dug grave, who took the piss when I shaved my head, who lied and said it was nice to see me. Who lied. And said it was nice to see me. I trusted you, I loved you, and it's not losing you that hurts me, but your bare-faced fucking falsehoods that masquerade as medical notes.

Your truth, your lies, not mine.

And while I was believing that you were different and that you maybe even felt the distress that sometimes flickered across your face and threatened to erupt, you were covering your arse too. Like every other stupid mortal cunt.

To my mind that's betrayal. And my mind is the subject of these bewildered fragments.

Nothing can extinguish my anger.

And nothing can restore my faith.

This is not a world in which I wish to live.

– – – – –

–   Have you made any plans?

–   Take an overdose, slash my wrists then hang myself.

–   All those things together?

–   It couldn't possibly be misconstrued as a cry for help.

     (*Silence.*)

–   It wouldn't work.

–   Of course it would.

–   It wouldn't work. You'd start to feel sleepy from the
    overdose and wouldn't have the energy to cut your
    wrists.

    (*Silence.*)

–   I'd be standing on a chair with a noose around my
    neck.

    (*Silence.*)

–   If you were alone do you think you might harm
    yourself?

–   I'm scared I might.

–   Could that be protective?

–   Yes. It's fear that keeps me away from the train tracks.
    I just hope to God that death is the fucking end. I feel
    like I'm eighty years old. I'm tired of life and my
    mind wants to die.

–   That's a metaphor, not reality.

–   It's a simile.

–   That's not reality.

–   It's not a metaphor, it's a simile, but even if it were,
    the defining feature of a metaphor is that it's real.

    (*A long silence.*)

–   You are not eighty years old.

    (*Silence.*)

Are you?

(*A silence.*)

Are you?

(*A silence.*)

Or are you?

(*A long silence.*)

–   Do you despise all unhappy people or is it me
    specifically?

–   I don't despise you. It's not your fault. You're ill.

–   I don't think so.

–   No?

–   No. I'm depressed. Depression is anger. It's what you
    did, who was there and who you're blaming.

–   And who are you blaming?

–   Myself.

– – – – –

Body and soul can never be married

I need to become who I already am and will bellow
forever at this incongruity which has committed me to
hell

Insoluble hoping cannot uphold me

I will drown in dysphoria
    in the cold black pond of my self
    the pit of my immaterial mind

How can I return to form
now my formal thought has gone?

Not a life that I could countenance.

They will love me for that which destroys me
    the sword in my dreams
    the dust of my thoughts
    the sickness that breeds in the folds of my mind

Every compliment takes a piece of my soul

An expressionist nag
Stalling between two fools
They know nothing –
    I have always walked free

Last in a long line of literary kleptomaniacs
    (a time honoured tradition)

Theft is the holy act
On a twisted path to expression

A glut of exclamation marks spells impending nervous
    breakdown
Just a word on a page and there is the drama

I write for the dead
    the unborn

After 4.48 I shall not speak again

I have reached the end of this dreary and repugnant
tale of a sense interned in an alien carcass and
lumpen by the malignant spirit of the moral majority

I have been dead for a long time

Back to my roots

I sing without hope on the boundary

– – – – –

RSVP ASAP

– – – – –

Sometimes I turn around and catch the smell of you and I
cannot go on I cannot fucking go on without expressing
this terrible so fucking awful physical aching fucking longing
I have for you. And I cannot believe that I can feel this for
you and you feel nothing. Do you feel nothing?

(*Silence.*)

Do you feel nothing?

(*Silence.*)

And I go out at six in the morning and start my search for
you. If I've dreamt a message of a street or a pub or a
station I go there. And I wait for you.

(*Silence.*)

You know, I really feel like I'm being manipulated.

(*Silence.*)

I've never in my life had a problem giving another person what they want. But no one's ever been able to do that for me. No one touches me, no one gets near me. But now you've touched me somewhere so fucking deep I can't believe and I can't be that for you. Because I can't find you.

(*Silence.*)

What does she look like?
And how will I know her when I see her?
She'll die, she'll die, she'll only fucking die.

(*Silence.*)

Do you think it's possible for a person to be born in the wrong body?

(*Silence.*)

Do you think it's possible for a person to be born in the wrong era?

(*Silence.*)

Fuck you. Fuck you. Fuck you for rejecting me by never being there, fuck you for making me feel shit about myself, fuck you for bleeding the fucking love and life out of me, fuck my father for fucking up my life for good and fuck my mother for not leaving him, but most of all, fuck you God for making me love a person who does not exist,
FUCK YOU FUCK YOU FUCK YOU.

– – – – –

—   Oh dear, what's happened to your arm?

—   I cut it.

—   That's a very immature, attention seeking thing to do. Did it give you relief?

—   No.

—   Did it relieve the tension?

—   No.

—   Did it give you relief?

    (*Silence.*)

    Did it give you relief?

—   No.

—   I don't understand why you did that.

—   Then ask.

—   Did it relieve the tension?

    (*A long silence.*)

    Can I look?

—   No.

—   I'd like to look, to see if it's infected.

—   No.

    (*Silence.*)

— I thought you might do this. Lots of people do. It relieves the tension.

— Have you ever done it?

— . . .

— No. Far too fucking sane and sensible. I don't know where you read that, but it does not relieve the tension.

(*Silence.*)

Why don't you ask me *why*?
Why did I cut my arm?

— Would you like to tell me?

— Yes.

— Then tell me.

— ASK.
ME.
WHY.

(*A long silence.*)

— Why did you cut your arm?

— Because it feels fucking great. Because it feels fucking amazing.

— Can I look?

— You can look. But don't touch.

— (*Looks*) And you don't think you're ill?

–   No.

–   I do. It's not your fault. But you have to take
    responsibility for your own actions. Please don't do it
    again.

– – – –

I dread the loss of her I've never touched
love keeps me a slave in a cage of tears
I gnaw my tongue with which to her I can never speak
I miss a woman who was never born
I kiss a woman across the years that say we shall never meet

> Everything passes
> Everything perishes
> Everything palls

> my thought walks away with a killing smile
> leaving discordant anxiety
> which roars in my soul

No hope No hope No hope No hope No hope No hope No hope

A song for my loved one, touching her absence
    the flux of her heart, the splash of her smile

In ten years time she'll still be dead. When I'm living with
it, dealing with it, when a few days pass when I don't even
think of it, she'll still be dead. When I'm an old lady living
on the street forgetting my name she'll still be dead, she'll
still be dead, it's just
                    fucking
                            over

                                    and I must stand alone

My love, my love, why have you forsaken me?

She is the couching place where I never shall lie
and there's no meaning to life in the light of my loss

>Built to be lonely
>to love the absent

>Find me
>Free me
>from this

>corrosive doubt
>futile despair

>horror in repose

>I can fill my space
>fill my time
>but nothing can fill this void in my heart

>The vital need for which I would die

>Breakdown

– – – – –

–   No ifs or buts.

–   I didn't say if or but, I said no.

—   Can't must never have-to always won't should shan't.
    The unnegotiables.
    Not today.

    (*Silence.*)

—   Please. Don't switch off my mind by attempting to
    straighten me out. Listen and understand, and when
    you feel contempt don't express it, at least not
    verbally, at least not to me.

    (*Silence.*)

—   I don't feel contempt.

—   No?

—   No. It's not your fault.

—   It's not your fault, that's all I ever hear, it's not your
    fault, it's an illness, it's not your fault, I know it's not
    my fault. You've told me that so often I'm beginning
    to think it *is* my fault.

—   It's *not* your fault.

—   I KNOW.

—   But you allow it.

    (*Silence.*)

    Don't you?

—   There's not a drug on earth can make life meaningful.

—   You allow this state of desperate absurdity.

    (*Silence.*)

You allow it.

(*Silence.*)

–   I won't be able to think. I won't be able to work.

–   Nothing will interfere with your work like suicide.

(*Silence.*)

–   I dreamt I went to the doctor's and she gave me eight minutes to live. I'd been sitting in the fucking waiting room half an hour.

(*A long silence.*)

Okay, let's do it, let's do the drugs, let's do the chemical lobotomy, let's shut down the higher functions of my brain and perhaps I'll be a bit more fucking capable of living.

Let's do it.

–   –   –   –   –

abstraction to the point of

unpleasant
unacceptable
uninspiring
impenetrable

irrelevant
irreverent
irreligious
unrepentant

dislike
dislocate
disembody
deconstruct

I don't imagine
  (clearly)
that a single soul
  could
    would
      should
        or will

and if they did
I don't think
  (clearly)
that another soul
a soul like mine
  could
    would
      should
        or will

irrespective

I know what I'm doing
  all too well

No native speaker

irrational
irreducible
irredeemable
unrecognisable

derailed
deranged
deform
free form

obscure to the point of

    True   Right   Correct
    Anyone or anybody
    Each   every   all

  drowning in a sea of logic
               this monstrous state of palsy

              still ill

          – – – –

Symptoms: Not eating, not sleeping, not speaking, no sex
drive, in despair, wants to die.

Diagnosis: Pathological grief.

Sertraline, 50 mg. Insomnia worsened, severe anxiety,
anorexia, (weight loss 17kgs,) increase in suicidal thoughts,
plans and intention. Discontinued following hospitalization.

Zopiclone, 7.5mg. Slept. Discontinued following rash.
Patient attempted to leave hospital against medical advice.
Restrained by three male nurses twice her size. Patient

threatening and uncooperative. Paranoid thoughts —
believes hospital staff are attempting to poison her.

Melleril, 50mg. Co-operative.

Lofepramine, 70mg, increased to 140mg, then 210mg.
Weight gain 12kgs. Short term memory loss. No other
reaction.

Argument with junior doctor whom she accused of
treachery after which she shaved her head and cut her
arms with a razor blade.

Patient discharged into the care of the community on
arrival of acutely psychotic patient in emergency clinic in
greater need of a hospital bed.

Citalopram, 20mg. Morning tremors. No other reaction.

Lofepramine and Citalopram discontinued after patient got
pissed off with side affects and lack of obvious improvement.
Discontinuation symptoms: Dizziness and confusion. Patient
kept falling over, fainting and walking out in front of cars.
Delusional ideas — believes consultant is the antichrist.

Fluoxetine hydrochloride, trade name Prozac, 20mg,
increased to 40mg. Insomnia, erratic appetite, (weight loss
14kgs,) severe anxiety, unable to reach orgasm, homicidal
thoughts towards several doctors and drug manufacturers.
Discontinued.

Mood: Fucking angry.
Affect: Very angry.

Thorazine, 100mg. Slept. Calmer.

Venlafaxine, 75mg, increased to 150mg, then 225mg.
Dizziness, low blood pressure, headaches. No other
reaction. Discontinued.

Patient declined Seroxat. Hypochondria – cites spasmodic
blinking and severe memory loss as evidence of tardive
dyskinesia and tardive dementia.

Refused all further treatment.

100 aspirin and one bottle of Bulgarian Cabernet
Sauvignon, 1986. Patient woke in a pool of vomit and said
'Sleep with a dog and rise full of fleas.' Severe stomach
pain. No other reaction.

– – – – –

Hatch opens
Stark light

        the television talks
        full of eyes
        the spirits of sight

                and now I am so afraid

        I'm seeing things
        I'm hearing things
        I don't know who I am

            tongue out
                    thought stalled

        the piecemeal crumple of my mind

Where do I start?
Where do I stop?
How do I start?
(As I mean to go on)

How do I stop?
How do I stop?
How do I stop?
How do I stop?
How do I stop?   A tab of pain
How do I stop?   Stabbing my lungs
How do I stop?   A tab of death
How do I stop?   Squeezing my heart

        I'll die
                not yet
                        but it's there

Please . . .
Money . . .
Wife . . .

Every act is a symbol
the weight of which crushes me

A dotted line on the throat
                CUT HERE

DON'T LET THIS KILL ME
THIS WILL KILL ME AND CRUSH ME AND
    SEND ME TO HELL

I beg you to save me from this madness that eats me
        a sub-intentional death

I thought I should never speak again
but now I know there is something blacker than desire

perhaps it will save me
perhaps it will kill me

a dismal whistle that is the cry of heartbreak around the
hellish bowl at the ceiling of my mind

a blanket of roaches

cease this war

My legs are empty
Nothing to say
And this is the rhythm of madness

– – – – –

– I gassed the Jews, I killed the Kurds, I bombed the
Arabs, I fucked small children while they begged for
mercy, the killing fields are mine, everyone left the
party because of me, I'll suck your fucking eyes out
send them to your mother in a box and when I die
I'm going to be reincarnated as your child only fifty
times worse and as mad as all fuck I'm going to make
your life a living fucking hell I REFUSE I REFUSE I
REFUSE LOOK AWAY FROM ME

– It's all right.

– LOOK AWAY FROM ME

—   It's all right. I'm here.

—   Look away from me

– – – – –

We are anathema
the pariahs of reason

Why am I stricken?
              I saw visions of God

and it shall come to pass

Gird yourselves:
for ye shall be broken in pieces
it shall come to pass

Behold the light of despair
the glare of anguish
and ye shall be driven to darkness

If there is blasting
              (there shall be blasting)
the names of offenders shall be shouted from the rooftops

Fear God
              and his wicked convocation

a scall on my skin, a seethe in my heart
a blanket of roaches on which we dance
this infernal state of siege

All this shall come to pass
all the words of my noisome breath

Remember the light and believe the light

Christ is dead
                    and the monks are in ecstasy

We are the abjects
who depose our leaders
and burn incense unto Baal

Come now, let us reason together
Sanity is found in the mountain of the Lord's house on the
    horizon of the soul that eternally recedes
The head is sick, the heart's caul torn
Tread the ground on which wisdom walks
Embrace beautiful lies –
    the chronic insanity of the sane

                              the wrenching begins

– – – – –

–   At 4.48
        when sanity visits
        for one hour and twelve minutes I am in my right mind.
        When it has passed I shall be gone again,
        a fragmented puppet, a grotesque fool.
        Now I am here I can see myself
        but when I am charmed by vile delusions of happiness,
        the foul magic of this engine of sorcery,
        I cannot touch my essential self.

        Why do you believe me then and not now?

        Remember the light and believe the light.
        Nothing matters more.
        Stop judging by appearances and make a right judgement.

–   It's all right. You will get better.

–   Your disbelief cures nothing.

    Look away from me.

                    – – – – –

Hatch opens
Stark light

A table two chairs and no windows

Here am I
and there is my body

                    dancing on glass

In accident time where there are no accidents

            You have no choice
            the choice comes after

Cut out my tongue
tear out my hair
cut off my limbs
but leave me my love
I would rather have lost my legs
pulled out my teeth
gouged out my eyes
than lost my love

flash   flicker   slash   burn   wring   press   dab   slash
flash   flicker   punch   burn   float   flicker   dab   flicker
punch   flicker   flash   burn   dab   press   wring   press
punch   flicker   float   burn   flash   flicker   burn

it will never pass

dab   flicker   punch   slash   wring   slash   punch   slash
float   flicker   flash   punch   wring   press   flash   press
dab   flicker   wring   burn   flicker   dab   flash   dab   float
burn   press   burn   flicker   burn   flash

Nothing's forever

(but Nothing)

slash   wring   punch   burn   flicker   dab   float   dab
flicker   burn   punch   burn   flash   dab   press   dab
wring   flicker   float   slash   burn   slash   punch   slash
press   slash   float   slash   flicker   burn   dab

Victim. Perpetrator. Bystander.

punch   burn   float   flicker   flash   flicker   burn   slash
wring   press   dab   slash   flash   flicker   dab   flicker
punch   flicker   flash   burn   dab   press   flicker   wring
press   punch   flash   flicker   burn   flicker   flash

the morning brings defeat

wring   slash   punch   slash   float   flicker   flash   punch
wring   dab   flicker   punch   slash   press   flash   press
dab   flicker   wring   burn   flicker   dab   flash   dab   float
burn   press   burn   flash   flicker   slash

                             beautiful pain
                                    that says I exist

flicker   punch   slash   dab   wring   press   burn   slash
press   slash   punch   flicker   flash   press   burn   slash
dab   flicker   float   flash   flicker   dab   press   burn   slash
press   slash   punch   flash   flicker   burn

                    and a saner life tomorrow

                    – – – –

           100
           93
           86
           79
           72
           65
           58
           51
           44
           37
           30
           23
           16
           9
           2

                              – – – –

Sanity is found at the centre of convulsion, where madness is scorched from the bisected soul.

I know myself.

I see myself.

My life is caught in a web of reason
        spun by a doctor to augment the sane.

At 4.48

                    I shall sleep.

I came to you hoping to be healed.

You are my doctor, my saviour, my omnipotent judge, my priest, my god, the surgeon of my soul.

And I am your proselyte to sanity.

– – – – –

to achieve goals and ambitions

to overcome obstacles and attain a high standard

to increase self-regard by the successful exercise of talent

to overcome opposition

to have control and influence over others

to defend myself

to defend my psychological space

to vindicate the ego

to receive attention

to be seen and heard

to excite, amaze, fascinate, shock, intrigue, amuse, entertain or entice others

to be free from social restrictions

to resist coercion and constriction

to be independent and act according to desire

to defy convention

to avoid pain

to avoid shame

to obliterate past humiliation by resumed action

to maintain self-respect

to repress fear

to overcome weakness

to belong

to be accepted

to draw close and enjoyably reciprocate with another

to converse in a friendly manner, to tell stories, exchange sentiments, ideas, secrets

to communicate, to converse

to laugh and make jokes

to win affection of desired Other

to adhere and remain loyal to Other

to enjoy sensuous experiences with cathected Other

to feed, help, protect, comfort, console, support, nurse or heal

to be fed, helped, protected, comforted, consoled, supported, nursed or healed

to form mutually enjoyable, enduring, cooperating and reciprocating relationship with Other, with an equal

to be forgiven

to be loved

to be free

— — — —

–   You've seen the worst of me.

–   Yes.

–   I know nothing of you.

–   No.

–   But I like you.

–   I like you.

   (*Silence.*)

–   You're my last hope.

   (*A long silence.*)

–   You don't need a friend you need a doctor.

   (*A long silence.*)

–   You are so wrong.

   (*A very long silence.*)

–   But you have friends.

   (*A long silence.*)

You have a lot of friends.
What do you offer your friends to make them so
supportive?

(*A long silence.*)

What do you offer your friends to make them so
supportive?

(*A long silence.*)

What do you offer?

(*Silence.*)

We have a professional relationship. I think we have a good relationship. But it's professional.

(*Silence.*)

I feel your pain but I cannot hold your life in my hands.

(*Silence.*)

You'll be all right. You're strong. I know you'll be okay because I like you and you can't like someone who doesn't like themself. The people I fear for are the ones I don't like because they hate themselves so much they won't let anyone else like them either. But I do like you. I'll miss you. And I know you'll be ok.

(*Silence.*)

Most of my clients want to kill me. When I walk out of here at the end of the day I need to go home to my lover and relax. I need to be with my friends and relax. I need my friends to be really together.

(*Silence.*)

I fucking hate this job and I need my friends to be sane.

(*Silence.*)

I'm sorry.

–   It's not my fault.

–   I'm sorry, that was a mistake.

–   It is not my fault.

–   No. It's not your fault. I'm sorry.

      (*Silence.*)

      I was trying to explain –

–   I know. I'm angry because I understand, not because I
      don't.

                          – – – –

Fattened up
  Shored up
    Shoved out

my body decompensates
my body flies apart

no way to reach out
beyond the reaching out I've already done

you will always have a piece of me
because you held my life in your hands

those brutal hands

this will end me

I thought it was silent
till it went silent

how have you inspired this pain?

I've never understood
what it is I'm not supposed to feel
like a bird on the wing in a swollen sky
my mind is torn by lightning
as it flies from the thunder behind

Hatch opens
Stark light
and Nothing
Nothing
see Nothing

What am I like?
                    the child of negation

out of one torture chamber into another
a vile succession of errors without remission
every step of the way I've fallen

Despair propels me to suicide
Anguish for which doctors can find no cure
Nor care to understand
I hope you never understand
Because I like you

I like you
I like you

still black water
as deep as forever
as cold as the sky
as still as my heart when your voice is gone
I shall freeze in hell

of course I love you
you saved my life

I wish you hadn't
I wish you hadn't
I wish you'd left me alone

a black and white film of yes or no yes or no yes or no yes
or no yes or no yes or no

I've always loved you
even when I hated you

What am I like?
just like my father

oh no oh no oh no

Hatch opens
Stark light

the rupture begins

I don't know where to look any more

Tired of crowd searching
Telepathy
and hope

Watch the stars
predict the past
and change the world with a silver eclipse

the only thing that's permanent is destruction
we're all going to disappear
trying to leave a mark more permanent than myself

I've not killed myself before so don't look for precedents
What came before was just the beginning

    a cyclical fear
    that's not the moon it's the earth
    A revolution

      Dear God, dear God, what shall I do?

    All I know
    is snow
          and black despair

    Nowhere left to turn
      an ineffectual moral spasm
      the only alternative to murder

Please don't cut me up to find out how I died
I'll tell you how I died

One hundred Lofepramine, forty five Zopiclone, twenty five
Temazepam, and twenty Melleril

Everything I had

Swallowed

Slit

Hung

It is done

    behold the Eunuch
      of castrated thought

    skull
    unwound

    the capture
     the rapture
      the rupture
       of a soul

    a solo symphony

    at 4.48
    the happy hour
    when clarity visits

    warm darkness
    which soaks my eyes

    I know no sin

    this is the sickness of becoming great

    this vital need for which I would die

to be loved

I'm dying for one who doesn't care
I'm dying for one who doesn't know

you're breaking me

Speak
Speak
Speak

ten yard ring of failure
look away from me

My final stand

No one speaks

Validate me
Witness me
See me
Love me

my final submission
my final defeat

the chicken's still dancing
the chicken won't stop

I think that you think of me
the way I'd have you think of me

the final period
the final full stop

look after your mum now
look after your mum

Black snow falls

in death you hold me

never free

I have no desire for death
no suicide ever had

watch me vanish
watch me

vanish

watch me

watch me

watch

It is myself I have never met, whose face is pasted on the underside of my mind

please open the curtains

– – – – –

9 780413 748300